WHSmith

Revise
English

KS2: YEAR 5

Age 9–10

Louis Fidge

First published 2007
exclusively for WHSmith by
Hodder Education, part of Hachette Livre UK,
338 Euston Road
London
NW1 3BH

Impression number   10 9 8 7 6 5 4 3 2
Year   2010 2009 2008
Text and illustrations © Hodder Education 2007

A CIP record for this book is available from the British Library.

Cover illustration by Sally Newton Illustrations

Typeset by Fakenham Photosetting Limited, Fakenham, Norfolk

ISBN   978 0 34094276 5

Printed and bound in Italy.

Contents

The *WHS Revise* series

The *WHS Revise* books enable you to help your child revise and practise important skills taught in school. These skills form part of the National Curriculum and will help your child to improve their Maths and English.

Testing in schools

During their time at school all children will undergo a variety of tests. Regular testing is a feature of all schools. It is carried out:

● *informally* – in everyday classroom activities your child's teacher is continually assessing and observing your child's performance in a general way
● *formally* – more regular formal testing helps the teacher check your child's progress in specific areas.

Testing is important because:

● it provides evidence of your child's achievement and progress
● it helps the teacher decide which skills to focus on with your child
● it helps compare how different children are progressing.

The importance of revision

Regular revision is important to ensure your child remembers and practises skills he or she has been taught. These books will help your child revise and test their knowledge of some of the things they will be expected to know. They will help you prepare your child to be in a better position to face tests in school with confidence.

How to use this book

Units

This book is divided into forty units, each focusing on one key skill. Each unit begins with a **Remember** section, which introduces and revises essential information about the particular skill covered. If possible, read and discuss this with your child to ensure he or she understands it.

This is followed by a **Have a go** section, which contains a number of activities to help your child revise the topic thoroughly and use the skill effectively. Usually, your child should be able to do these activities fairly independently.

Revision tests

There are four revision tests in this book (pages 46–53). These test the skills covered in the preceding units and assess your child's progress and understanding. They can be marked by you or by your child. Your child should fill in his or her test score for each test in the space provided. This will provide a visual record of your child's progress and an instant sense of confidence and achievement.

Parents' notes

The parents' notes (on pages 54–57) provide you with brief information on each skill and explain why it is important.

Answers

Answers to the unit questions and tests may be found on pages 58–64.

Unit 1: Homophones

Remember

Homophones are words that **sound the same**, but are **spelt differently** and have **different meanings**.

On **board** ship I was very **bored**.

Have a go

1 Match up the pairs of homophones.

weight   weather   meet   new   prey   blue   sleigh   pale

meat   pray   blew   wait   slay   pail   whether   knew

2 Choose the correct homophone to complete each sentence.

a The man let out a loud _____ . (groan/grown)

b The _____ of the sun were bright. (raise/rays)

c The _____ ran across the field. (hair/hare)

d The _____ family went on holiday. (hole/whole)

e I wasn't sure _____ was my drink. (which/witch)

f We paid our _____ on the bus. (fare/fair)

g The lion caught its _____ . (pray/prey)

h The ball broke the _____ of glass. (pain/pane)

Unit 2: Auxiliary verbs

Remember

Sometimes we need an **extra verb** to help the main verb make sense.

These verbs are called **auxiliary** (or **helper**) verbs.

The pirate **is** burying some treasure.

Have a go

1 Underline the auxiliary verb in each sentence.

a Anna is writing a letter.

b The man was mending the car.

c I am swimming in the sea.

d The children were fighting.

e I will call for you tomorrow.

f I have been to a party.

g Sarah can speak French.

h I do know the way.

2 Choose the correct auxiliary verb to complete each sentence.

a James _____ waiting for his results. (is, are)

b I _____ going on holiday soon. (am, are)

c You _____ see the moon on a clear night. (does, can)

d Mary _____ been to sleep. (has, have)

e What _____ the teacher do? (were, did)

f _____ you think it is fair? (Do, Shall)

g The cars _____ travelling too fast. (was, were)

h Why _____ it always rain so much? (do, does)

i Next week I _____ having a party. (will, am)

j _____ you stand on your head? (Can, Does)

Unit 3: Letter patterns

Remember

It is helpful to look for **common letter patterns** in groups of words.

This can help us remember their spellings.

share

care

square

Have a go

Make new words using the same letter patterns. Read them aloud.

a
Change the **c** in **c**are to **d, sc, bew, prep**.

dare _____   _____   _____

b
Change the **h** in **h**ere to **w, m, wh, th**.

_____   _____   _____   _____

c
Change the **w** in **w**ire to **h, f, sp, requ**.

_____   _____   _____   _____

d
Change the **s** in **s**ore to **st, sc, bef, expl**.

_____   _____   _____   _____

e
Change the **c** in **c**ure to **s, sec, end, meas**.

_____   _____   _____   _____

Unit 4: Adverbs (1)

Remember

An **adverb** tells us more about a **verb**. Adverbs often tell us **how** something happened. Many adverbs end in **ly**.

The lion roared **loudly**.

Have a go

1 Underline the adverb in each sentence.

a The stars shone brightly that night.

b The boy spoke politely to the visitor.

c Time passed quickly.

d We solved the problem easily.

e Silently, the thief opened the door.

f I splashed happily in the water.

g Do your writing neatly.

h Are you sitting comfortably?

2 Choose the best adverb to complete each sentence.

> tidily generously wearily quietly sadly gently patiently bravely

a The soldier fought _____ .

b The children whispered _____ .

c The girl folded her clothes _____ .

d The man gave _____ to the beggar.

e The tired lady sat down _____ .

f The child cried _____ .

g The girl waited _____ for the bus.

h Tom stroked the cat _____ .

Unit 5: Synonyms

Remember

Synonyms are words with **similar** meanings.

cross

angry

Have a go

Match up the pairs of synonyms.

Write the words here.

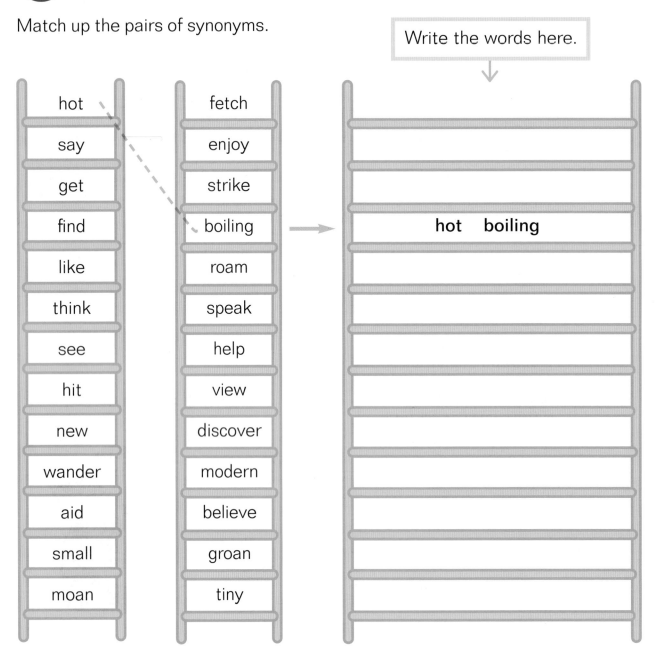

hot	fetch
say	enjoy
get	strike
find	boiling
like	roam
think	speak
see	help
hit	view
new	discover
wander	modern
aid	believe
small	groan
moan	tiny

hot   boiling

Unit 6: Common and proper nouns

Remember

A **common noun** is a **naming** word. It may be the name of a **person**, **place** or **thing**.

A **proper noun** is the **particular** name of a person, place or thing. Proper nouns begin with **capital** letters.

woman   supermarket   trolley

My name is **C**laire.
I live in **S**windon.

Have a go

1 Underline the common nouns.
   Say if each noun is the name of a person, place or thing.

    (person)   (thing)
   a A <u>pilot</u> flies an <u>aeroplane</u>.   b A garage is for cars.

   c A reporter writes for a newspaper. d A library is for books.

   e A florist sells flowers.   f A bank is for money.

   g A tailor makes clothes.   h A harbour is for ships.

2 Rewrite these sentences. Begin each proper noun with a capital letter.

   a ben nevis is a mountain in scotland. _____

   b cardiff is the capital of wales. _____

   c my birthday is in march not may. _____

   d sir francis drake was an explorer. _____

   e we stayed in the star hotel in madrid. _____

   f we arrived at heathrow airport in london. _____

 **Remember**

We use many **common expressions** in our language.
Sometimes they are a little hard to understand!
For example, if we give away a secret we say we are
letting the cat out of the bag!

 **Have a go**

1 Match up these sayings to the pictures. Write them on the first line.

| to rain cats and dogs | to take the bull by the horns |

| to be under a cloud | to sit on the fence |

a

to take the bull by the horns
_____

b

_____
_____

c

_____
_____

d

_____
_____

2 Now write the real meaning of each saying on the second line.

| to meet dangers boldly | to be under suspicion |

| to refuse to take sides | to rain heavily |

Unit 8: Adjectives

Remember

An **adjective** is a **describing** word. It gives us more **information about a noun**.

a **hot** drink on a **cold** day

Have a go

Write the words here.

1 Match up the pairs of opposite adjectives.

foolish	shallow
blunt	full
deep	wise
rough	expensive
empty	sharp
bent	smooth
cheap	light
heavy	straight

_____

_____

foolish   wise

_____

_____

_____

_____

2 Reorder these adjectives in order of intensity.

a	chilly	cold	lukewarm
b	hot	tepid	warm
c	high	low	medium
d	damp	wet	dry
e	clean	dirty	spotless
f	hard	firm	soft
g	grey	white	black
h	deafening	quiet	noisy

a	**cold**	**chilly**	**lukewarm**
b			
c			
d			
e			
f			
g			
h			

Remember

A **prefix** is a group of letters that goes **in front** of a word. Prefixes change the **meanings** of words.

visible   —   **in**visible

Have a go

❶ Add the prefixes to make new words.

a

a

board → **aboard**

loft → _____

shore → _____

sleep → _____

waken → _____

b

be

friend → _____

come → _____

loved → _____

little → _____

side → _____

❷ Use the words you made.

a _____ means up high

b _____ means to start being something

c _____ is the opposite of praise

d _____ is the opposite of to make enemies

e _____ means next to

f _____ means to wake up

g _____ is the opposite of awake

h _____ means on board

i _____ means on the shore

j _____ means much loved

Remember

A simple **sentence** is always made up of **two** parts:
the **subject** (who or what the sentence is about)
the **predicate** (the rest of the sentence, including the verb).

(verb)
⬇
The wind **blew** strongly.
⬆   ⬆
(subject)   (predicate)

Have a go

1 Underline the subject and circle the predicate in each sentence.

a <u>The angry dog</u> (barked loudly.)   b The greedy boy ate the cake.

c The shopkeeper counted the money.   d The best team won the cup.

e Submarines travel underwater.   f The sea was very rough.

g We like swimming.   h The moon came out.

2 Join up each subject with a suitable predicate.

subjects	predicates
The sun	went to bed early.
Uncle Ben	was very untidy.
The tired boy	slithered through the grass.
Some brave mountaineers	shone very brightly.
My handwriting	skidded on some oil.
The snake	came to visit me.
The sports car	turned brown.
The leaves	reached the summit.

Unit 11: Tricky spellings (1)

Remember

a w**ar**m w**or**m

| When **ar** follows **w** it often sounds like **or**. | When **or** follows **w** it often sounds like **er**. |

Have a go

① Write these words in the table below.

> warm   worm   world   reward   swarm
> worse   work   warn   ward   worth

ar words (sound like **or**)	**or** words (sound like **er**)

② Choose from the words above to complete these sentences.

a All _____ and no play makes Jack a dull boy.

b The _____ is the planet on which we live.

c It is _____ in the summer.

d Ten tens are _____ a hundred.

e To _____ someone is to tell them of danger.

f A group of bees is called a _____.

g Mary's writing seems to get _____ rather than better!

h You are sometimes given a _____ for helping someone.

i When I was in hospital I stayed in a _____.

j The early bird catches the _____.

Unit 12: Pronouns (1)

Remember

A **pronoun** is a word that **takes the place of a noun**.

Tom got hurt when **he** (Tom) fell off **it** (Tom's bike).

Have a go

1 Choose the best pronoun to complete each sentence.

a (They, It) _____ is very misty today.

b When the man stood up, (he, she) _____ fell over.

c Are (it, you) _____ able to come out tonight?

d (I, You) _____ am very hungry.

e The boy spoke to the lady and asked (him, her) _____ the time.

f I like Jamie but (we, he) _____ does not like (us, me) _____ .

g "Will (they, you) _____ be quiet, please?" Mr Jones asked.

2 Write who or what each underlined pronoun stands for.

a The lady picked up the case and carried <u>it</u> (_____) to the car.

b Emma has a pet rabbit. <u>She</u> (_____) looks after <u>it</u> (_____) very well.

c "<u>I</u> (_____) like football," Wayne said.

d "Let <u>us</u> (_____) help <u>you</u> (_____)," Edward and Tom said to Cara.

e Sam wanted to play with her friends but <u>they</u> (_____) were not in.

f "Are <u>you</u> (_____) coming or not?" Mrs Allen asked Dan and Rosie.

g The man tried to move the rock but <u>it</u> (_____) was too heavy for <u>him</u> (_____).

Unit 13: Suffixes – *al* and *ful*

Remember

A **suffix** is a group of letters that can be added to the end of a word to **change its meaning** or the **way it is used**.

help + **ful** = helpful   music + **al** = musical

Have a go

① Choose the suffix **al** or **ful** to complete each word.

a comic____   b help____   c accident____   d season_____   e use_____

f care____   g tropic____   h stress____   i nation____   j power____

② Write the words you made in the table below.

al words	**ful** words

③ Take the suffix off each word. Write the root word you are left with. Note that the spelling of the root word will sometimes change slightly.

a beauti~~ful~~   **beauty**   b natural   _____

c central   _____   d faithful   _____

e restful   _____   f industrial   _____

g continental   _____   h skilful   _____

i plentiful   _____   j personal   _____

Unit 14: Direct speech

Remember

When we write down the words a person actually says, we call this **direct speech**. We put the words they actually say inside **speech marks**. When a **new speaker** begins we should begin a **new line**.

 What's for tea?   It's fish fingers.

"What's for tea?" Jack asked.
"It's fish fingers," his mum replied.

Have a go

1 Put in the missing speech marks in these sentences.

a I don't like custard! Amy exclaimed.

b I can't do it! William shouted.

c Kyle asked, What is the time?

d It's cold outside, Shannon said.

e Let's go shopping, suggested Paul.

f Tell me a story, the toddler begged.

g Close your books, the teacher ordered.

h The magician exclaimed, Abracadabra!

2 Rewrite the following passage in direct speech.
Start a new line for each new speaker.

I feel ill! Sarah exclaimed. Do you want to go to bed? her mother asked. Sarah replied, I'll see how I feel later. Her mother said, Shall I telephone the doctor? I'm not that ill! Sarah answered. In that case, you can go to school, her mother said.

_____

_____

_____

_____

_____

Unit 15: Spelling rules (1)

When adding a suffix to a **single-syllable word**, ending with a **short vowel and a consonant**, we **double** the **final consonant** before adding the suffix.

run   run + **ing** = ru**nn**ing   run + **er** = ru**nn**er
(root word)   (root word + different suffixes)

Complete these tables.

verb	+ suffix ing	+ suffix ed
wag	**wagging**	**wagged**
stop		
tug		
rob		
chat		
beg		
ban		
jog		
pop		

adjective	+ suffix er	+ suffix est
wet	**wetter**	**wettest**
big		
hot		
thin		
fit		
sad		
dim		
mad		
fat		

Unit 16: Punctuation (1)

 **Remember**

Punctuation marks help the reader **make sense** of a text.

have you seen the eiffel tower ☒
This is not punctuated correctly.

Have you seen the Eiffel Tower? ☑
This is correct. It is easier to read.

 **Have a go**

Copy these sentences and punctuate them correctly.
Put in the capital letters, full stops, question and exclamation marks.

a   did you know that camels are found in africa

_____

b   we saw newcastle united play on saturday

_____

c   what a lovely surprise

_____

d   mrs barnes is rich but mr peters is richer

_____

e   do you prefer pizza or spaghetti

_____

f   last year i went to greece for my holiday

_____

g   i think sprouts are awful

_____

h   mr smith is always quarrelling with his wife

_____

i   kennedy airport is in new york

_____

j   his birthday was the last saturday in april

_____

Unit 17: Standard English (1)

Remember

Standard English is the kind of language you are expected to use in school. The **subject** (the main person or thing) and **verb** in every sentence must always **agree**.

The duck **were** grumpy. ☒   The duck **was** grumpy. ☑

Have a go

1 Use **was** or **were** to complete each sentence.

a It _____ raining hard.

b The birds _____ chirping in the trees.

c The hippo _____ drinking at the river.

d We _____ going to see my uncle.

e The crocodile _____ asleep.

f You _____ wrong.

g _____ it too hard for you?

h _____ the bees buzzing loudly?

2 Choose the correct form of the verb to complete each sentence.

a He _____ the book for us to see. (bring, brought)

b They _____ away each weekend. (go, goes)

c Toby _____ some tricks with a ball. (did, done)

d They _____ very good apples. (wasn't, weren't)

e Our teacher _____ us a test. (give, gave)

f He _____ a lot to do. (has, have)

g Who _____ you talking to? (was, were)

h When I was late I _____ to school. (run, ran)

i Last week I _____ the queen. (saw, seen)

◯ Remember

We are always **changing** and **adapting** our language.
Sometimes we **shorten** words, or use **abbreviations**.

bike becomes the word for **bicycle**

PTO means **please turn over**

◯ Have a go

① Join up each short word with the longer word from which it comes.

② Join up each abbreviation with its meaning.

short form	longer form	abbreviation	meaning
bike	laboratory	PTO	United States of America
plane	omnibus	DOB	Post Office
lab	bicycle	PO	United Nations
phone	refrigerator	UK	please turn over
bus	canister	USA	World Health Organisation
pram	aeroplane	UN	Greenwich Mean Time
fridge	submarine	HQ	date of birth
vet	telephone	GMT	headquarters
sub	perambulator	MP	United Kingdom
can	veterinarian	WHO	Member of Parliament

Unit 19: Conjunctions (1)

Remember

We can use a **conjunction** (a **joining** word) to join two sentences together to make one longer sentence.

The woman went into the shop. She bought a new dress.
The woman went into the shop **where** she bought a new dress.

Have a go

1 Match up the beginning and ending of these long sentences.

a	I don't like apples	when he got lost.
b	My teacher was happy	after I had been to Italy.
c	The man asked the way	because I was muddy.
d	Everyone cheered	before I went to bed.
e	I watched TV	when I got my spellings right.
f	I visited France	because I scored a goal.
g	I had a bath	although it was raining.
h	I went out	so I only eat bananas.

2 Write the sentences you made. Underline the conjunction in each. The first is done for you.

a   I don't like apples <u>so</u> I only eat bananas.

b _____

c _____

d _____

e _____

f _____

g _____

h _____

Unit 20: Alphabetical order

Remember

Dictionaries are organised in **alphabetical order**.

These words are organised according to the **third** letter.

These words are organised according to the **fourth** letter.

Have a go

Write each set of words in alphabetical order.

a | coconut
confuse
comic
coat

_____   _____   _____   _____

b | hiss
hill
hiccup
hinge

_____   _____   _____   _____

c | last
lace
label
lantern

_____   _____   _____   _____

d | shore
shop
shoot
shoe

_____   _____   _____   _____

e | mark
march
marble
marvel

_____   _____   _____   _____

f | ransack
rank
ranch
random

_____   _____   _____   _____

Unit 21: Homonyms

Remember

A **homonym** is a word with the **same spelling** as another but with a **different meaning**.

I went for a walk with my **mummy**.

Have a go

1 Underline the homonyms in these pairs of sentences.

a I gave my mum a wave.   The big wave splashed all over me.

b It is wrong to tell a lie.   I could lie in bed all day.

c I looked inside the old wooden   The gorilla thumped its chest
   chest.   angrily.

d The petrol tank was empty.   The army tank was very noisy.

e The box was too heavy to lift.   I took the lift to the top floor.

f I spread some jam on my bread.   The car was stuck in a traffic jam.

2 Make up pairs of sentences using the homonyms below. Remember the homonym must have a different meaning in each sentence.

match _____

_____

dress _____

_____

play _____

_____

tie _____

_____

Unit 22: Verb tenses

Remember

Yesterday I **played** football.

Now I **am playing** tennis.

Tomorrow I **will play** cricket.

This happened in the **past**.
The verb is in the **past tense**.

This is happening **now**.
The verb is in the **present tense**.

This will happen in the **future**.
The verb is in the **future tense**.

Have a go

1 Complete the table.

verb	present tense	past tense	future tense
crawl	I am crawling	I crawled	I will crawl
dance	I am dancing		
hop	I am hopping		
jump		I jumped	
try			

2 Change the verbs from the past tense to the future tense.

a I got up late.　　　　　　　　**I will get up late.**

b I ate my lunch.　　　　　　　_____

c I watched cartoons on TV.　_____

d Then I telephoned my friend.　_____

e After this I rode to Sam's house.　_____

Unit 23: More letter patterns

Remember

It is helpful to look for **common letter patterns** in groups of words. This can help us remember their spellings.

collec**tion**

The **tion** at the end of a word sounds like **shun**.

explo**sion**

The **sion** at the end of a word sounds like **zhun**.

Have a go

1 Join up each **tion** noun with the verb from which it comes.

direction	act
creation	collect
action	direct
education	protect
collection	create
protection	educate
imagination	generate
preparation	inspect
generation	imagine
separation	decorate
inspection	prepare
decoration	separate

2 Join up each **sion** noun with the verb from which it comes.

inclusion	confuse
confusion	divide
decision	explode
erosion	decide
division	include
television	invade
explosion	erode
invasion	televise
revision	conclude
conclusion	provide
provision	deride
derision	revise

Unit 24: Adverbs (2)

An **adverb** tells us more about a **verb**.
Adverbs often tell us **how** something happened. Many adverbs end in **ly**.

The crowd cheered **enthusiastically**.

1 Replace the adverb in each sentence with an adverb from the box which means the same.

crossly	happily	tidily	senselessly	unkindly	quickly

   a Vicky laughed (cheerfully) _____.

   b I behaved (stupidly) _____ at the match.

   c The woman treated the dog (cruelly) _____.

   d I always write (neatly) _____.

   e The man shouted (angrily) _____.

   f I did my homework (hurriedly) _____.

2 Underline the odd one out in each set of adverbs.

   a   secretly   furtively   loudly   sneakily

   b   keenly   usually   eagerly   enthusiastically

   c   expertly   fearlessly   gallantly   bravely

   d   carefully   warily   awkwardly   cautiously

   e   fairly   cunningly   slyly   craftily

   f   foolishly   equally   stupidly   senselessly

   g   pleasantly   charmingly   sweetly   shabbily

   h   nervously   angrily   worriedly   anxiously

Unit 25: Antonyms

Remember

| Synonyms are words with similar meanings. | Antonyms are words with opposite meanings. |

jovial   jolly

empty   full

Have a go

1 Replace the word in brackets. Make the new sentence mean the opposite.

a Finally the train (departed) _____.

b The small boy was very (weak) _____.

c The woman was full of (hatred) _____.

d The (interior) _____ of the house was badly decorated.

e The prisoner was found (guilty) _____.

f The attempt to reach the summit was a (failure) _____.

2 Underline the antonym in each set for the word on the left.

a	dirty	muddy	<u>clean</u>	grubby	big
b	high	wide	up	drop	low
c	foolish	wise	silly	wet	red
d	polite	sensible	nice	rude	easy
e	gentle	painful	caring	calm	rough
f	humble	proud	down	huge	tall

Unit 26: Collective nouns

Remember

A **collective** noun is a **group** or **collection** of people or things.

a **choir** of singers

a **flock** of sheep

Have a go

1 Complete each phrase correctly with a noun from the box.

flock	herd	pack	shoal	crew	band
school	collection	fleet	litter	swarm	gaggle

a a _____ of cows   b a _____ of wasps

c a _____ of cards   d a _____ of stamps

e a _____ of birds   f a _____ of puppies

g a _____ of fish   h a _____ of dolphins

i a _____ of ships   j a _____ of sailors

k a _____ of geese   l a _____ of pirates

2 Choose the best word to complete each collective noun.

a a (flock, string) _____ of beads

b a (gang, swarm) _____ of thieves

c a (set, bundle) _____ of sticks

d a (bunch, beach) _____ of bananas

e a (bouquet, smell) _____ of flowers

f a (grab, clutch) _____ of eggs

g a (crow, crowd) _____ of people

h a (bride, pride) _____ of lions

Unit 27: Common expressions (2)

Remember

We use many **common expressions** in our language.
Sometimes they are a little hard to understand!
For example, in a heavy rainfall we might say that
it's raining cats and dogs!

Match up each common expression with its real meaning.

to bury the hatchet	to be a spoilsport
to be a wet blanket	to do something for yourself
to hit below the belt	to keep a secret
to paddle your own canoe	to boast about yourself
to send someone to Coventry	to settle a quarrel
to keep it in the dark	to start afresh
to turn over a new leaf	to act unfairly
to hang your head	to be suspicious
to smell a rat	not to speak to someone
to blow your own trumpet	to be ashamed

Unit 28: Comparative and superlative

Remember

When we compare **two** nouns we use a **comparative adjective**.
When we compare **more than two** nouns we use a **superlative adjective**.

My face is **muddy**.

↑

This is the
root adjective.

My face is **muddier**.

↑

Comparative adjectives
often end with **er**.

My face is the **muddiest**.

↑

Superlative adjectives
often end with **est**.

Have a go

1 Complete this table. Watch the spellings!

root adjective	comparative adjective	superlative adjective
tall	taller	
wide		widest
hot		
dry		driest
	sharper	
		wettest
	happier	
		largest
strange		
	thinner	
		heaviest

2 In the sentences below, underline the comparative adjectives and circle the superlative adjectives.

a A rhinoceros is fat. A hippo is fatter but an elephant is the fattest.

b Sam has the fastest bike. It is faster than mine.

c The river was wider near the bend.

d The aliens were stronger, fiercer and taller than humans.

e The blue bag was the cheapest. It was cheaper than the orange one.

f The first ape was hairy. The next one was hairier. The last one was the hairiest thing I have ever seen!

Remember

A **prefix** is a group of letters that goes **in front** of a word.
Prefixes change the **meanings** of words.

behave

misbehave

Have a go

1. Do these prefix sums.

   a up + bringing = _____

   b dis + appear = _____

   c ex + port = _____

   d for + give = _____

   e mid + day = _____

   f re + call = _____

   g after + noon = _____

   h bi + sect = _____

   i un + clear = _____

   j pre + dict = _____

   k mis + behave = _____

   l with + hold = _____

2. Choose the correct prefix to give each word the opposite meaning.

   a

in	un

   unreliable

   b

dis	mis

   ___fortune

   c

in	dis

   ___complete

   d

mis	un

   ___pleasant

   e

in	mis

   ___lead

   f

in	im

   ___patient

   g

il	ir

   ___legal

   h

il	ir

   ___regular

   i

in	mis

   ___capable

   j

un	mis

   ___inform

   k

in	im

   ___mature

   l

il	ir

   ___logical

Unit 30: Sentences and phrases

Remember

Sarah fell into a muddy puddle.

↑

This is a **sentence**.
A sentence **makes sense** on its own.
A sentence always contains a **verb**.

into a muddy puddle

↑

This is a **phrase**.
It does **not** make sense on its own.
It is a group of words **without** a verb.
Phrases are usually **short**.

Have a go

1 Say if each of these is a sentence (S) or a phrase (P).

a Many caterpillars are green. (__)   b Snails live in shells. (__)

c in the garden (__)   d small insects (__)

e A spider has eight legs. (__)   f a silver web (__)

g like a worm (__)   h Ants live underground. (__)

2 Choose a suitable phrase to complete each sentence.

in a spaceship   during the spring   through the streets   with one blow
small bears   like a fish   black clouds   with a broken pencil

a The sky was full of _____.

b The man knocked in the nail _____.

c The band marched _____.

d You can't draw _____.

e _____ trees begin to bud.

f Sam can swim _____.

g _____ are called cubs.

h The aliens landed _____.

Unit 31: Tricky spellings (2)

 **Remember**

Sometimes the **o** in a word sounds like **u**.

a m**o**nkey wearing gl**o**ves

Have a go

1 Make some words. Read the words you make.

o

n_o_ne	n__thing	m__nth	m__ney	d__zen	fr__nt
none	_____	_____	_____	_____	_____

o

l__ve	m__nk	w__nder	s__mething	inc__me	t__ngue
_____	_____	_____	_____	_____	_____

o

sp__nge	s__me	am__ng	s__n	sh__ve	h__ney
_____	_____	_____	_____	_____	_____

2 Write the word or words you made which rhymes with:

a hum   _____   b bunk   _____

c funny _____   d fun   _____

e plunge _____   f cousin _____

g shunt _____   h thunder _____

Unit 32: Pronouns (2)

Remember

1. We use **1st person pronouns** like **I** and **we** when we write about **ourselves**.
   When **I** met Sam **we** shared some sweets.

2. When we write **to others** we use **2nd person pronouns** like **you**.
   When **you** come bring your swimming trunks with **you**.

3. When we write **about others** we use **3rd person pronouns** like **he**, **she**, **it** and **they**.
   Tom startled the dog. **It** barked at **him**.

Have a go

1. Write whether each underlined pronoun is the 1st or 2nd person.

   a <u>I</u> (**1st**) went shopping.

   b <u>We</u> (____) bought some crisps.

   c <u>You</u> (_____) must not play in the road.

   d Where are <u>you</u> (_____)?

   e May <u>I</u> (___) come with <u>you</u> (___)?

   f Why are <u>you</u> (___) sad?

   g Come with <u>us</u> (___).

   h <u>We</u> (___) live here.

2. This passage is written in the 3rd person. Underline the pronouns in it.

   Sarah does not like swimming. She likes the beach but she does not feel safe in the sea. The thought of fishes near her scares her. Once a crab bit her toe when she was paddling. She has never been the same since!

3. Now write the passage in the 1st person as if you were Sarah. Do it like this:

<u>**I do not like swimming.**</u> _____

_____

_____

_____

Remember

A **suffix** is a group of letters that can be added to the **end** of a word to **change its meaning** or the **way it is used**.

affection (noun)   affection**ate** (adjective)

Have a go

1 Join up each noun to the adjective which may be made from it.

Write them here.

noun	adjective
affection	crafty
child	energetic
craft	affectionate
expense	comfortable
energy	childish
favour	furious
comfort	favourite
fury	expensive

_____

_____

__affection – affectionate__

_____

_____

_____

_____

_____

2 Take the suffix off each adjective. Write the noun you are left with. Note that the spelling of the noun will sometimes change slightly.

adjective	noun
marvellous	**marvel**
boyish	
metallic	
cowardly	
heroic	
faithful	

adjective	noun
golden	
furry	
athletic	
mountainous	
fortunate	
natural	

Unit 34: Direct and reported speech

Remember

We can write speech as **direct** or **reported** (**indirect**) speech.

The boy said, "I can run very fast."   The boy said that he could run very fast.

This is written in **direct speech**. The **exact** words spoken are inside **speech marks**.

This is written in **reported** (**indirect**) speech. The boy's exact words are **not used**, nor are speech marks.

Have a go

1 Put in the speech marks in these sentences written in direct speech. Then write each sentence in reported (indirect) speech.

   a   The boy said, "I can't swim."   __The boy said that he couldn't swim.__

   b   I'm the best speller, the girl boasted.   _____

   c   I feel worn out, Dionne complained.   _____

   d   James asked, Why are you all late?   _____

   e   Stop it! shouted Cara to James.   _____

2 After each sentence say if it is written in **direct** (D) or **reported** (R) speech.

   a   "I want some new trainers," said Harry. (___)

   b   Mary said that she had a new coat. (___)

   c   Paul said that he watched television last night. (___)

   d   "What have you found?" asked Joanne. (___)

   e   "My car is broken," Mr Brown explained. (___)

   f   The doctor said, "You've got the measles." (___)

Unit 35: Spelling rules (2)

Remember

When adding a suffix **beginning with a vowel** to a short word ending with a **magic e**, we usually **drop** the **e before** adding the suffix.

bake   bake + **ing** = baking   bake + **ed** = baked   bake + **er** = baker

Have a go

1 Add the suffix **ing** to each of these words.

a make   <u>making</u>   b glide   _____   c smile   _____

d give   _____   e hope   _____   f hate   _____

g note   _____   h shove   _____   i whine   _____

2 Write a word you made above that rhymes with:

a sliding   _____   b grating   _____   c dining   _____

d voting   _____   e baking   _____   f living   _____

g loving   _____   h filing   _____   i sloping   _____

3 Take the suffix off each word. Write the root word you are left with.

a diver   <u>dive</u>   b scorer   _____   c blazer   _____

d joker   _____   e manager   _____   f racer   _____

g stranger _____   h skater   _____   i diner   _____

j waved   _____   k refused   _____   l chased   _____

m excited   _____   n deserved _____   o droned   _____

p fumed   _____   q bribed   _____   r chimed   _____

Unit 36: Punctuation (2)

Remember

Punctuation marks help the reader make sense of a text.

Heres my car Sarah Tom said.

"Here's my car, Sarah," Tom said.

↑

This is not punctuated correctly.

↑

This is correct. It is easier to read.

Have a go

Copy these sentences and punctuate them correctly.
All the commas, apostrophes and speech marks have been left out.

a   Mount Everest the tallest mountain in the world towered above us.

_____

b   Come here Dan Sarah said.

_____

c   The old van all rusty and muddy stopped outside.

_____

d   The child whispered Lets get out of here!

_____

e   Mr Jones said Good morning Doctor Brown.

_____

f   After a while Sam appeared and said Its time for dinner.

_____

Unit 37: Standard English (2)

Remember

Standard English is the kind of language you are expected to use in school. A common mistake is to include **double negatives** in sentences.

I didn't see nothing. ☒

↑

This sentence contains a **double negative**.

I didn't see anything. ☑

↑

This sentence is **correctly** written.

Have a go

1 Tick the sentences that are correct. Cross those which are wrong.

a I haven't got no money. ☐   b That is not right. ☐

c I can't do anything. ☐   d The girl didn't say nothing. ☐

e I never hurt nobody. ☐   f I have not seen anyone. ☐

g I have not been anywhere. ☐   h I didn't go nowhere nice. ☐

2 Write each sentence in correct standard English.

a There isn't no point going out.   b I don't want no beans.

_____   _____

c He wasn't nowhere near me.   d I don't play no sports.

_____   _____

e A snake hasn't got no legs.   f The man didn't say nothing.

_____   _____

g I never do nothing wrong.   h The woman never saw nobody.

_____   _____

i I couldn't find the map nowhere.   j I haven't never been to New York.

_____   _____

Remember

Over the years we have **borrowed** many words from **other languages**, including French.

a bouquet of flowers   a trumpet

Have a go

1 Complete these French words we use. Which do we pronounce **ay**?

et

duv**et**   trump__   banqu__   sach__   ball__

et

scarl__   brack__   bouqu__   cabar__   blank__

2 Complete these sentences with the words you made.

a   A _____ is a large feast held on special occasions.

b   _____ is a bright red colour.

c   A _____ is a bunch of flowers.

d   A _____ is a musical instrument.

e   A _____ is a variety of different entertainments.

f   _____ is a kind of dancing.

g   A _____ is a small packet.

h   A _____ is a bed covering filled with feathers.

i   A _____ is used to hold up a shelf.

j   A _____ is a bed covering that goes over a sheet.

 **Remember**

We can use a **conjunction** (a **joining** word) to join two sentences together to make one longer sentence.

> I tried not to cry. My knee really hurt.
> I tried not to cry **although** my knee really hurt.

 **Have a go**

Choose **although**, **because** or **as** to join these pairs of sentences. Write each pair as one long sentence.

a   There was a traffic jam. There had been an accident.

_____

b   Ben did not eat his dinner. He was very hungry.

_____

c   Everybody liked Joanne. She was a good sport.

_____

d   The striker headed the ball. The referee blew his whistle.

_____

e   We managed to reach the island. The ship was letting in water.

_____

f   Mr Smith was reading the newspaper. He was eating his breakfast.

_____

g   I arrived at school. My teacher was calling the register.

_____

h   The police hurried to the scene. They were too late to catch the robber.

_____

Unit 40: Dictionary work – definitions

Remember

Dictionaries help us find out the definitions (meanings) of words.

zoom   to move very quickly

Have a go

Use a dictionary to help you complete this A–Z of definitions.

a_ _ _ _ _   someone who draws or paints
b_ _ _   a hollow piece of metal that rings when hit
c_ _ _ _ _   a big gun that fires heavy metal balls
d_ _ _ _   a male duck
e_ _   a type of tree
f_ _   healthy
g_ _   a valuable or beautiful stone
h_ _ _ _   a kind of wall made with bushes
i_ _   frozen water
j_ _   to run slowly
k_ _ _ _ _   the middle part of a nut
l_ _ _   a young sheep
m_ _ _ _   to chew noisily
n_ _ _ _   the noise a horse makes
o_ _ _   to leave out
p_ _ _   a juicy fruit grown on a tree
q_ _ _ _   without noise
r_ _   to tear
s_ _   the liquid inside a plant
t_ _ _ _   shy, not brave
u_ _ _ _ _   not smooth or level
v_ _ _ _   not clear or certain
w_ _ _ _ _   to shake like a jelly
x-_ _ _   a photograph of the inside of the body
y_ _ _   the yellow part of an egg
z_ _ _   the number nought

Test 1

Check how much you have learned.

Answer the questions.
Mark your answers. Fill in your score.

1   Underline the pair of homophones in each set.

a | rein   ruin   ream   reign |

b | soon   sun   son   sum |

out of 2

2   Choose the correct auxiliary verb to complete each sentence.

a   The children _____ going swimming.
    (are, did)

b   _____ you want to come? (Can, Do)

out of 2

3   Think of two words which contain the **ape** letter pattern.

a   _____   b   _____

out of 2

4   Underline the adverb in each sentence.

a   The puppy ate its food greedily.

b   Quietly the girl sat down.

out of 2

5   Think of a synonym with three letters to go with each word.

a   enquire   ___ ___ ___

b   peculiar   ___ ___ ___

out of 2

6   Underline the common noun and circle the proper noun in this sentence:

Vicky got out her book.

out of 2

7 Tick the correct meaning of each common expression.

a **It's raining cats and dogs.**

It's raining heavily. ☐

It's drizzling. ☐

b **to face the music**

to play a musical instrument ☐

to accept punishment without complaint ☐

out of 2

☐

8 These two adjectives mean the opposite. Fill in the missing letters.

a cl__ __ n   b d __ __ ty

out of 2

☐

9 Choose the prefix **a** or **be** to begin each word.

a ____friend   b ____board

out of 2

☐

10 Underline the subject and circle the predicate in the sentence.

An owl hunts at night.

out of 2

☐

Total out of 20

☐

Test 2

Check how much you have learned.

Answer the questions.
Mark your answers. Fill in your score.

SCORE

1 Complete each word correctly.

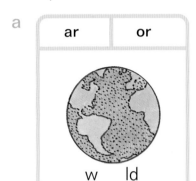

a
ar	or

w___ld

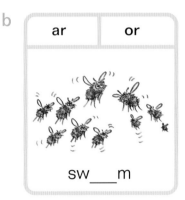

b
ar	or

sw___m

out of 2

2 Say who each underlined pronoun refers to.

a Amy made a drink when <u>she</u> (_____) got home.

b "How are <u>you</u> (_____)?" the teacher asked James.

out of 2

3 Choose the suffix **ful** or **al** to complete each word.

a accident____   b rest____

out of 2

4 Fill in the missing speech marks.

a Where shall we go? Charlotte asked.

b Sarah replied, Let's go shopping.

out of 2

5 Add the suffixes. Spell the words correctly.

a swim + ing = _____

b slip + er = _____

out of 2

6 Rewrite this sentence and punctuate it correctly.

What is the capital of france

_____

out of 2

7 Choose the auxiliary verb **was** or **were** to complete each sentence correctly.

a Some horses _____ galloping.

b Each dog _____ barking.

8 a Write the short form of **omnibus**. _____

out of 2

b Write the abbreviation for **United Kingdom**.
_____

9 Underline the conjunction in each sentence.

out of 2

a I stood at the front so I could see better.

b I washed my hands before I ate my dinner.

10 Write each set of words in alphabetical order.

a flush

flour _____ _____ _____

flint

b brook

out of 2

brother _____ _____ _____

broad

Total out of 20

49

Test 3

Check how much you have learned.

Answer the questions.
Mark your answers. Fill in your score.

1 Use the same word to complete each sentence.

a The football team played in an exciting _____ .

b I struck a _____ to light the candle.

out of 2

2 Fill in the chart correctly.

verb	present tense	past tense	future tense
skip	I am skipping	I skipped	I _____
rake	I am raking	I _____	I will rake

out of 2

3 Complete each word correctly.

a

tion		sion

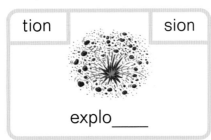

explo____

b

tion		sion

collec____

out of 2

4 Replace the adverb in each sentence with either **enthusiastically** or **neatly**, to mean the same.

a I folded up my clothes <u>tidily</u> (_____).

b I put my hand up <u>eagerly</u> (_____).

out of 2

5 Think of a five-letter antonym for each word.

a long   <u>s</u> <u>h</u> __ __ __

b whisper   <u>s</u> <u>h</u> __ __ __

out of 2

6 Choose the correct collective noun for each phrase.

a a (pack, litter) _____ of puppies

b a (fleet, shoal) _____ of ships

7 Tick the correct meaning of each expression.

a to turn over a new leaf:

to look for something under a leaf ☐

to start afresh ☐

b to smell a rat:

to be suspicious ☐

to find a rats' nest ☐

8 Complete this table.

root adjective	comparative form	superlative form
happy	happier	
sad		saddest

9 Begin each word with the correct prefix.

a

for		re

____give

b

con		ex

____pand

10 Say if each of these is a sentence (S) or a phrase (P).

a a hard shell   (___)

b A tortoise has a hard shell.   (___)

Test 4

Check how much you have learned.

Answer the questions.
Mark your answers. Fill in your score.

SCORE

1 Spell each word correctly.

    a nuthing _____   b frunt _____

out of 2

2 Say if the underlined pronoun is in the 1st, 2nd or 3rd person.

    a Can <u>you</u> come here for a moment?   (__)

    b <u>They</u> searched everywhere for the missing money. (__)

out of 2

3 Take the suffix off each adjective. Write the noun you are left with.

    a comfortable _____   b childish _____

out of 2

4 Say if each sentence is written in direct (D) or reported (R) speech.

    a "What a lovely day!" Mrs Jones exclaimed.   (__)

    b Mr Jones said that he would cut the grass.   (__)

out of 2

5 Add the suffixes. Spell the words correctly.

    a hope + ing = _____   b manage + er = _____

out of 2

6 Fill in the missing punctuation marks.

Wheres my towel Amy Tom asked.

out of 2

7 Rewrite each sentence correctly.

a I can't see no sweets.

_____

b I never hurt no-one.

_____

8 Tick the correct definition for each word.

a ballet   a kind of dance   ☐

                a small ball   ☐

b trumpet   a musical instrument   ☐

                a card game   ☐

9 Underline the conjunction in each sentence.

a Anna did not stop although she wanted to.

b Anna rushed home because she was late.

10 Complete the word for each definition.

a f_____   the coat of a sheep

b g_____   a very strong wind

Parents' notes

Unit 1: Homophones   Words that sound the same but have different meanings are called homophones. ('Homo' means 'the same' and 'phone' means 'sound'.) Encourage your child to use a dictionary to check the correct spelling if in doubt.

Unit 2: Auxiliary verbs   Sometimes a verb needs an additional verb to help it work properly e.g. I **can** knit, I **am** going, I **do** know. These extra verbs are called auxiliary (or helper) verbs.

Unit 3: Letter patterns   There are many common letter patterns (letters which frequently come together) in words. It is important for your child to recognise these when reading and to be able to use them when writing. The letter patterns **are**, **ere**, **ire**, **ore** and **ure** are the focus of this unit.

Unit 4: Adverbs (1)   Remind your child that an adverb tells us more about a verb. Many adverbs (adverbs of manner) tell us about how something happened. Many of these adverbs end with the suffix **ly**.

Unit 5: Synonyms   Synonyms are words which have the same, or very similar meanings. Using synonyms makes our writing more interesting and adds variety. Encourage your child to use a thesaurus if you have one.

Unit 6: Common and proper nouns   Remind your child that nouns (or naming words) may be the name of a person, place or thing. A noun is called a common noun if it refers to the general name of the object e.g. town. A noun is called a proper noun if it refers to the name of a particular person, place or thing e.g. London. Proper nouns always begin with a capital letter.

Unit 7: Common expressions (1)   We use lots of colloquial expressions, idioms and sayings, whose meanings might be difficult for your child to understand, since they are usually not intended to be taken literally.

Unit 8: Adjectives   Remind your child that an adjective is a describing word. It tells us more about a noun. Adjectives help us make our writing more interesting and descriptive.

Unit 9: Prefixes – *a* and *be*   A prefix is a group of letters we can add to the front of a word. Prefixes change the meaning of the word. The addition of the prefixes **a** and **be** are the focus of this unit.

Unit 10: Sentences – subject and predicate   A sentence should make sense on its own and must always contain a verb. A simple sentence always consists of two parts: the subject (who or what the sentence is about) and the predicate (the rest of the sentence, including the verb).

Unit 11: Tricky spellings (1) It is helpful to provide your child with simple rules to help him or her understand the spelling of some tricky words. When **ar** follows the letter **w** it often sounds like **or**, as in w**ar**m. When **or** follows the letter **w** it often sounds like **er** as in w**or**d.

Unit 12: Pronouns (1) Remind your child that a pronoun is a word that takes the place of a noun. ('Pro' actually means 'in place of'.) We use pronouns to avoid a lot of repetition in sentences. Personal pronouns take the place of the names of people or things e.g. Tom bought a comic when he (Tom) went out.

Unit 13: Suffixes – *al* and *ful* A suffix is a group of letters we add to the end of a word. Your child needs to understand that many words may be extended by adding suffixes. Adding a suffix changes the meaning of the word in some way. In this unit the suffixes **al** and **ful** are the focus. Point out to your child that there is only a single **l** at the end of each when used as a suffix.

Unit 14: Direct speech When we write down what people say, we use speech marks. Remind your child that the words a person says should go inside the speech marks. Note that every time someone different speaks, we should begin a new line.

Unit 15: Spelling rules (1) Much of our spelling system is governed by logical rules. Understanding these can help your child develop sound spelling strategies. The spelling rule focused on here is that when we add a suffix to a single-syllable word, ending with a short vowel and a consonant, we double the final consonant before adding the suffix e.g. run + ing = running.

Unit 16: Punctuation (1) Punctuation marks make writing easier for us to understand. They are essential for meaning. The activities focus on the use of capital letters, full stops, question and exclamation marks in sentences.

Unit 17: Standard English (1) Standard English is the kind of language your child is expected to use in school. We often use non-standard English informally when speaking. This unit focuses on ensuring that the subject (the main person or thing) and verb of each sentence agree.

Unit 18: Our living language (1) Our language never stands still. We are continually adding to it or modifying it in some way. This unit looks at the way we commonly shorten longer words or abbreviate them.

Unit 19: Conjunctions (1) Remind your child that a conjunction is a joining word which may be used to join two sentences together. (Help your child to remember this by likening it to a road junction, where two roads join together.) This page features several common conjunctions.

Unit 20: Alphabetical order A dictionary is a very valuable tool for a child. Your child needs to know how to use one. This page focuses on understanding alphabetical order, according to the third and fourth letters of words.

Unit 21: Homonyms Words that are spelt the same but have different meanings are called homonyms. ('Homo' means 'the same'.) Encourage your child to use a dictionary to check multiple meanings of words.

Unit 22: Verb tenses Verbs may be written in different tenses. When a verb tells of an action taking place now, we say that it is written in the present tense. A verb describing an action which has already taken place is written in the past tense e.g. Last week I **bought** a new car. A verb describing something that will happen in the future is written in the future tense e.g. Tomorrow I **will go** into town.

Unit 23: More letter patterns The letter patterns **tion** and **sion** are the focus of this unit.

Unit 24: Adverbs (2) Many adverbs (adverbs of manner) tell us about how something happened. Many of these adverbs end with the suffix **ly**. This unit provides more work on adverbs of manner.

Unit 25: Antonyms Synonyms are words which have the same, or very similar meanings. Antonyms are words with opposite meanings.

Unit 26: Collective nouns A collective noun is the name given to a group or collection of things or people e.g. a choir of singers, a fleet of ships.

Unit 27: Common expressions (2) This unit extends the work of Unit 7.

Unit 28: Comparative and superlative When we compare two nouns we use a comparative adjective. Comparative adjectives often end in **er** e.g. sweeter. When we compare more than two nouns we use a superlative adjective. These often end in **est** e.g. sweetest.

Unit 29: More about prefixes A variety of different prefixes are featured in this unit.

Unit 30: Sentences and phrases A sentence should make sense on its own and must always contain a verb. A phrase, on the other hand, does not make sense on its own and does not usually contain a verb e.g. a big, black car. Phrases tend to be shorter than sentences.

Unit 31: Tricky spellings (2)   It is helpful to provide your child with simple rules to help him or her understand the spelling of some tricky words. The words in this unit all contain the letter **o** which sounds like a letter **u** e.g. money.

Unit 32: Pronouns (2)   Pronouns may be written in the 1st person when we write about ourselves (e.g. I, me, we, us). 2nd person pronouns are used when we write to others (e.g. you). We use 3rd person pronouns (e.g. he, she, it, they) when we write about others.

Unit 33: More about suffixes   In this unit we look at how some nouns may be changed into adjectives by the addition of suffixes.

Unit 34: Direct and reported speech   We may write down speech in two ways – as direct or reported (indirect) speech. In direct speech we enclose what the person says inside speech marks e.g. Sam said, "I like Tom." In reported speech we report what the person says without using speech marks e.g. Sam said that he likes Tom.

Unit 35: Spelling rules (2)   The spelling rule focused on in this unit is that when we add a suffix beginning with a vowel to a short word ending with a **magic e**, we usually drop the **e** before adding the suffix e.g. make + ing = making.

Unit 36: Punctuation (2)   The activities in this unit focus on the use of commas, apostrophes and speech marks in sentences.

Unit 37: Standard English (2)   We often hear grammatically incorrect sentences being spoken. The use of double negatives is a common mistake e.g. I didn't see no-one.

Unit 38: Our living language (2)   Our language never stands still. We are continually adding to it by borrowing words from other languages. This unit looks at some French words which we now commonly use.

Unit 39: Conjunctions (2)   This unit features several more common conjunctions.

Unit 40: Dictionary work – definitions   This unit focuses on the function of the dictionary for providing definitions of words.

Answers

Unit 1: Homophones (page 6)

1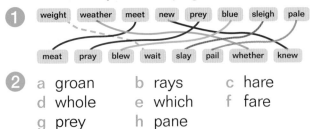

weight · weather · meet · new · prey · blue · sleigh · pale

meat · pray · blew · wait · slay · pail · whether · knew

2
a groan	b rays	c hare
d whole	e which	f fare
g prey	h pane	

Unit 2: Auxiliary verbs (page 7)

1
a Anna <u>is</u> writing a letter.
b The man <u>was</u> mending the car.
c I <u>am</u> swimming in the sea.
d The children <u>were</u> fighting.
e I <u>will</u> call for you tomorrow.
f I <u>have</u> been to a party.
g Sarah <u>can</u> speak French.
h I <u>do</u> know the way.

2
a is	b am	c can
d has	e did	f Do
g were	h does	i am
j Can		

Unit 3: Letter patterns (page 8)

a dare	scare	beware	prepare
b were	mere	where	there
c hire	fire	spire	require
d store	score	before	explore
e sure	secure	endure	measure

Unit 4: Adverbs (1) (page 9)

1
a The stars shone <u>brightly</u> that night.
b The boy spoke <u>politely</u> to the visitor.
c Time passed <u>quickly</u>.
d We solved the problem <u>easily</u>.
e <u>Silently</u>, the thief opened the door.
f I splashed <u>happily</u> in the water.
g Do your writing <u>neatly</u>.
h Are you sitting <u>comfortably</u>?

2
a bravely	b quietly
c tidily	d generously
e wearily	f sadly
g patiently	h gently

Unit 5: Synonyms (page 10)

get	fetch
like	enjoy
hit	strike
hot	boiling
wander	roam
say	speak
aid	help
see	view
find	discover
new	modern
think	believe
moan	groan
small	tiny

Unit 6: Common and proper nouns (page 11)

1
a A <u>pilot</u> flies an <u>aeroplane</u>.
   (person)   (thing)
b A <u>garage</u> is for <u>cars</u>.
   (place)   (thing)
c A <u>reporter</u> writes for a <u>newspaper</u>.
   (person)   (thing)
d A <u>library</u> is for <u>books</u>.
   (place)   (thing)
e A <u>florist</u> sells <u>flowers</u>.
   (person)   (thing)
f A <u>bank</u> is for <u>money</u>.
   (place)   (thing)
g A <u>tailor</u> makes <u>clothes</u>.
   (person)   (thing)
h A <u>harbour</u> is for <u>ships</u>.
   (place)   (thing)

2
a Ben Nevis is a mountain in Scotland.
b Cardiff is the capital of Wales.
c My birthday is in March not May.
d Sir Francis Drake was an explorer.
e We stayed in the Star Hotel in Madrid.
f We arrived at Heathrow Airport in London.

Unit 7: Common expressions (1) (page 12)

1
a to take the bull by the horns
b to sit on the fence
c to rain cats and dogs
d to be under a cloud

2
a to meet dangers boldly
b to refuse to take sides
c to rain heavily
d to be under suspicion

Unit 8: Adjectives (page 13)

1
deep	shallow
empty	full
foolish	wise
cheap	expensive
blunt	sharp
rough	smooth
heavy	light
bent	straight

2
a   cold   chilly   lukewarm
b   tepid   warm   hot
c   low   medium   high
d   dry   damp   wet
e   dirty   clean   spotless
f   soft   firm   hard
g   white   grey   black
h   quiet   noisy   deafening
(Some could be in opposite order!)

Unit 9: Prefixes – *a* and *be* (page 14)

1
a	**a**board	b	**be**friend
	aloft		**be**come
	ashore		**be**loved
	asleep		**be**little
	awaken		**be**side

2
a   aloft   b   become
c   belittle   d   befriend
e   beside   f   awaken
g   asleep   h   aboard
i   ashore   j   beloved

Unit 10: Sentences – subject and predicate (page 15)

1
a   <u>The angry dog</u> barked loudly .
b   <u>The greedy boy</u> ate the cake .
c   <u>The shopkeeper</u> counted the money .
d   <u>The best team</u> won the cup .
e   <u>Submarines</u> travel underwater .
f   <u>The sea</u> was very rough .
g   <u>We</u> like swimming .
h   <u>The moon</u> came out .

2
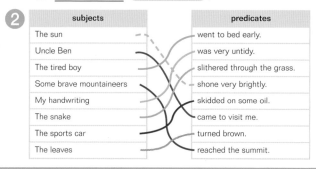

subjects	predicates
The sun	went to bed early.
Uncle Ben	was very untidy.
The tired boy	slithered through the grass.
Some brave mountaineers	shone very brightly.
My handwriting	skidded on some oil.
The snake	came to visit me.
The sports car	turned brown.
The leaves	reached the summit.

Unit 11: Tricky spellings (1) (page 16)

1
ar words (sound like **or**)	**or** words (sound like **er**)
warm	worm
reward	world
swarm	worse
warn	work
ward	worth

2
a   work   b   world   c   warm
d   worth   e   warn   f   swarm
g   worse   h   reward   i   ward
j   worm

Unit 12: Pronouns (1) (page 17)

1
a   It   b   he   c   you
d   I   e   her   f   he/me
g   you

2
a   the case
b   Emma/the rabbit
c   Wayne
d   Edward and Tom/Cara
e   Sam's friends
f   Dan and Rosie
g   the rock/the man

Unit 13: Suffixes – *al* and *ful* (page 18)

1
a   comical   b   helpful
c   accidental   d   seasonal
e   useful   f   careful
g   tropical   h   stressful
i   national   j   powerful

2
al words	**ful** words
comical	helpful
accidental	useful
seasonal	careful
tropical	stressful
national	powerful

3
a   beauty   b   nature
c   centre   d   faith
e   rest   f   industry
g   continent   h   skill
i   plenty   j   person

Unit 14: Direct speech (page 19)

1
a   "I don't like custard!" Amy exclaimed.
b   "I can't do it!" William shouted.
c   Kyle asked, "What is the time?"
d   "It's cold outside," Shannon said.
e   "Let's go shopping," suggested Paul.
f   "Tell me a story," the toddler begged.

g "Close your books," the teacher ordered.

h The magician exclaimed, "Abracadabra!"

2 "I feel ill!" Sarah exclaimed.
"Do you want to go to bed?" her mother asked.
Sarah replied, "I'll see how I feel later."
Her mother said, "Shall I telephone the doctor?"
"I'm not that ill!" Sarah answered.
"In that case, you can go to school," her mother said.

Unit 15: Spelling rules (1) (page 20)

verb	+ suffix ing	+ suffix ed
wag	wagging	wagged
stop	stopping	stopped
tug	tugging	tugged
rob	robbing	robbed
chat	chatting	chatted
beg	begging	begged
ban	banning	banned
jog	jogging	jogged
pop	popping	popped

adjective	+ suffix er	+ suffix est
wet	wetter	wettest
big	bigger	biggest
hot	hotter	hottest
thin	thinner	thinnest
fit	fitter	fittest
sad	sadder	saddest
dim	dimmer	dimmest
mad	madder	maddest
fat	fatter	fattest

Unit 16: Punctuation (1) (page 21)

a Did you know that camels are found in Africa?

b We saw Newcastle United play on Saturday.

c What a lovely surprise!

d Mrs Barnes is rich but Mr Peters is richer.

e Do you prefer pizza or spaghetti?

f Last year I went to Greece for my holiday.

g I think sprouts are awful!

h Mr Smith is always quarrelling with his wife.

i Kennedy Airport is in New York.

j His birthday was the last Saturday in April.

Unit 17: Standard English (1) (page 22)

1 a was   b were   c was
d were   e was   f were
g Was   h Were

2 a brought   b go   c did
d weren't   e gave   f has
g were   h ran   i saw

Unit 18: Our living language (1) (page 23)

1

short form	longer form
bike	laboratory
plane	omnibus
lab	bicycle
phone	refrigerator
bus	canister
pram	aeroplane
fridge	submarine
vet	telephone
sub	perambulator
can	veterinarian

2
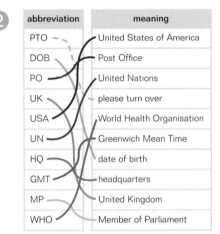

abbreviation	meaning
PTO	United States of America
DOB	Post Office
PO	United Nations
UK	please turn over
USA	World Health Organisation
UN	Greenwich Mean Time
HQ	date of birth
GMT	headquarters
MP	United Kingdom
WHO	Member of Parliament

Unit 19: Conjunctions (1) (page 24)

1

a I don't like apples — when he got lost.
b My teacher was happy — after I had been to Italy.
c The man asked the way — because I was muddy.
d Everyone cheered — before I went to bed.
e I watched TV — when I got my spellings right.
f I visited France — because I scored a goal.
g I had a bath — although it was raining.
h I went out — so I only eat bananas.

2 a I don't like apples so I only eat bananas.

b My teacher was happy when I got my spellings right.

c The man asked the way when he got lost.

d Everyone cheered because I scored a goal.

e I watched TV before I went to bed.

f I visited France after I had been to Italy.

g I had a bath because I was muddy.

h I went out although it was raining.

Unit 20: Alphabetical order (page 25)

a coat   coconut   comic   confuse
b hiccup   hill   hinge   hiss
c label   lace   lantern   last
d shoe   shoot   shop   shore
e marble   march   mark   marvel
f ranch   random   rank   ransack

Unit 21: Homonyms (page 26)

1
a I gave my mum a <u>wave</u>.
   The big <u>wave</u> splashed all over me.
b It is wrong to tell a <u>lie</u>.
   I could <u>lie</u> in bed all day.
c I looked inside the old wooden <u>chest</u>.
   The gorilla thumped its <u>chest</u> angrily.
d The petrol <u>tank</u> was empty.
   The army <u>tank</u> was very noisy.
e The box was too heavy to <u>lift</u>.
   I took the <u>lift</u> to the top floor.
f I spread some <u>jam</u> on my bread.
   The car was stuck in a traffic <u>jam</u>.

2 Check each sentence is correct and that the homonyms have a different meaning in each sentence.

Unit 22: Verb tenses (page 27)

1

verb	present tense	past tense	future tense
crawl	I am crawling	I crawled	I will crawl
dance	I am dancing	I danced	I will dance
hop	I am hopping	I hopped	I will hop
jump	I am jumping	I jumped	I will jump
try	I am trying	I tried	I will try

2
a I will get up late.
b I will eat my lunch.
c I will watch cartoons on TV.
d Then I will telephone my friend.
e After this I will ride to Sam's house.

Unit 23: More letter patterns (page 28)

1

Unit 24: Adverbs (2) (page 29)

1
a happily   b senselessly
c unkindly   d tidily
e crossly   f quickly

2
a secretly   furtively   <u>loudly</u>   sneakily
b keenly   <u>usually</u>   eagerly   enthusiastically
c <u>expertly</u>   fearlessly   gallantly   bravely
d carefully   warily   <u>awkwardly</u>   cautiously
e <u>fairly</u>   cunningly   slyly   craftily
f foolishly   <u>equally</u>   stupidly   senselessly
g pleasantly   charmingly   sweetly   <u>shabbily</u>
h nervously   <u>angrily</u>   worriedly   anxiously

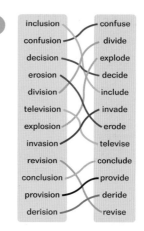

Unit 25: Antonyms (page 30)

1
a arrived   b strong
c love   d exterior
e innocent   f success

2

a dirty	muddy	<u>clean</u>	grubby	big
b high	wide	up	drop	<u>low</u>
c foolish	<u>wise</u>	silly	wet	red
d polite	sensible	nice	<u>rude</u>	easy
e gentle	painful	caring	calm	<u>rough</u>
f humble	<u>proud</u>	down	huge	tall

Unit 26: Collective nouns (page 31)

1
a herd   b swarm
c pack   d collection
e flock   f litter
g shoal   h school
i fleet   j crew
k gaggle   l band

2
a string   b gang
c bundle   d bunch
e bouquet   f clutch
g crowd   h pride

Unit 27: Common expressions (2) (page 32)

to bury the hatchet	to be a spoilsport
to be a wet blanket	to do something for yourself
to hit below the belt	to keep a secret
to paddle your own canoe	to boast about yourself
to send someone to Coventry	to settle a quarrel
to keep it in the dark	to start afresh
to turn over a new leaf	to act unfairly
to hang your head	to be suspicious
to smell a rat	not to speak to someone
to blow your own trumpet	to be ashamed

Unit 28: Comparative and superlative (page 33)

1

root adjective	comparative adjective	superlative adjective
tall	taller	tallest
wide	wider	widest
hot	hotter	hottest
dry	drier	driest
sharp	sharper	sharpest
wet	wetter	wettest
happy	happier	happiest
large	larger	largest
strange	stranger	strangest
thin	thinner	thinnest
heavy	heavier	heaviest

2
a A rhinoceros is fat. A hippo is <u>fatter</u> but an elephant is the (fattest).
b Sam has the (fastest) bike. It is <u>faster</u> than mine.
c The river was <u>wider</u> near the bend.
d The aliens were <u>stronger</u>, <u>fiercer</u> and <u>taller</u> than humans.
e The blue bag was the (cheapest). It was <u>cheaper</u> than the orange one.
f The first ape was hairy. The next one was <u>hairier</u>. The last one was the (hairiest) thing I have ever seen!

Unit 29: More about prefixes (page 34)

1
a upbringing
b disappear
c export
d forgive
e midday
f recall
g afternoon
h bisect
i unclear
j predict
k misbehave
l withhold

2
a unreliable
b misfortune
c incomplete
d unpleasant
e mislead
f impatient
g illegal
h irregular

i incapable
j misinform
k immature
l illogical

Unit 30: Sentences and phrases (page 35)

1
a S   b S   c P   d P
e S   f P   g P   h S

2
a black clouds
b with one blow
c through the streets
d with a broken pencil
e during the spring
f like a fish
g small bears
h in a spaceship

Unit 31: Tricky spellings (2) (page 36)

1 n**o**ne n**o**thing m**o**nth m**o**ney d**o**zen fr**o**nt l**o**ve m**o**nk w**o**nder s**o**mething inc**o**me t**o**ngue sp**o**nge s**o**me am**o**ng s**o**n sh**o**ve h**o**ney

2
a some   b monk
c money or honey   d son
e sponge   f dozen
g front   h wonder

Unit 32: Pronouns (2) (page 37)

1
a 1st   b 1st   c 2nd
d 2nd   e 1st/2nd   f 2nd
g 1st   h 1st

2 Sarah does not like swimming. <u>She</u> likes the beach but <u>she</u> does not feel safe in the sea. The thought of fishes near <u>her</u> scares <u>her</u>. Once a crab bit her toe when <u>she</u> was paddling. <u>She</u> has never been the same since!

3 I do not like swimming. I like the beach but I do not feel safe in the sea. The thought of fishes near me scares me. Once a crab bit my toe when I was paddling. I have never been the same since!

Unit 33: More about suffixes (page 38)

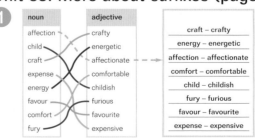

noun	adjective
affection	crafty
child	energetic
craft	affectionate
expense	comfortable
energy	childish
favour	furious
comfort	favourite
fury	expensive

craft – crafty
energy – energetic
affection – affectionate
comfort – comfortable
child – childish
fury – furious
favour – favourite
expense – expensive

adjective	noun
marvellous	marvel
boyish	boy
metallic	metal
cowardly	coward
heroic	hero
faithful	faith

adjective	noun
golden	gold
furry	fur
athletic	athlete
mountainous	mountain
fortunate	fortune
natural	nature

Unit 34: Direct and reported speech (page 39)

1
a The boy said, "I can't swim."
The boy said that he couldn't swim.
b "I'm the best speller," the girl boasted.
The girl boasted that she was the best speller.
c "I feel worn out," Dionne complained.
Dionne complained that she felt worn out.
d James asked, "Why are you all late?"
James asked why they were all late.
e "Stop it!" shouted Cara to James.
Cara shouted to James to stop it.

2 a D   b R   c R   d D
e D   f D

Unit 35: Spelling rules (2) (page 40)

1 a making   b gliding   c smiling
d giving   e hoping   f hating
g noting   h shoving   i whining

2 a gliding   b hating   c whining
d noting   e making   f giving
g shoving   h smiling   i hoping

3 a dive   b score   c blaze
d joke   e manage   f race
g strange   h skate   i dine
j wave   k refuse   l chase
m excite   n deserve   o drone
p fume   q bribe   r chime

Unit 36: Punctuation (2) (page 41)

a Mount Everest, the tallest mountain in the world, towered above us.
b "Come here, Dan," Sarah said.
c The old van, all rusty and muddy, stopped outside.
d The child whispered, "Let's get out of here!"
e Mr Jones said, "Good morning, Doctor Brown."
f After a while, Sam appeared and said, "It's time for dinner."

Unit 37: Standard English (2) (page 42)

1
a I haven't got no money. ✗
b That is not right. ✓
c I can't do anything. ✓
d The girl didn't say nothing. ✗
e I never hurt nobody. ✗
f I have not seen anyone. ✓
g I have not been anywhere. ✓
h I didn't go nowhere nice. ✗

2 Other wordings are possible.
a There isn't any point going out.
b I don't want any beans.
c He wasn't anywhere near me.
d I don't play any sports.
e A snake hasn't got any legs.
f The man didn't say anything.
g I never do anything wrong.
h The woman never saw anybody.
i I couldn't find the map anywhere.
j I haven't ever been to New York.

Unit 38: Our living language (2) (page 43)

1 Those in bold are said **ay**.
du**vet**   trumpet   ban**quet**   sach**et**
ballet   scarlet   bracket   bou**quet**
cabar**et**   blanket

2 a banquet   b Scarlet
c bouquet   d trumpet
e cabaret   f Ballet
g sachet   h duvet
i bracket   j blanket

Unit 39: Conjunctions (2) (page 44)

a There was a traffic jam **because** there had been an accident.
b Ben did not eat his dinner **although** he was very hungry.
c Everybody liked Joanne **because** she was a good sport.
d The striker headed the ball **as** the referee blew his whistle.
e We managed to reach the island **although** the ship was letting in water.
f Mr Smith was reading the newspaper **as** he was eating his breakfast.
g I arrived at school **as** my teacher was calling the register.
h The police hurried to the scene **although** they were too late to catch the robber.

Unit 40: Dictionary work – definitions (page 45)

artist	someone who draws or paints
bell	a hollow piece of metal that rings when hit
cannon	a big gun that fires heavy metal balls
drake	a male duck
elm	a type of tree
fit	healthy
gem	a valuable or beautiful stone
hedge	a kind of wall made with bushes
ice	frozen water
jog	to run slowly
kernel	the middle part of a nut
lamb	a young sheep
munch	to chew noisily
neigh	the noise a horse makes
omit	to leave out
pear	a juicy fruit grown on a tree
quiet	without noise
rip	to tear
sap	the liquid inside a plant
timid	shy, not brave
uneven	not smooth or level
vague	not clear or certain
wobble	to shake like a jelly
x-ray	a photograph of the inside of the body
yolk	the yellow part of an egg
zero	the number nought

Test 1 (pages 46 and 47)

1. a <u>rein</u> <u>reign</u>
   b <u>sun</u> <u>son</u>
2. a are   b Do
3. There are a number of possible answers. Examples include shape, tape, gape, cape.
4. a The puppy ate its food <u>greedily</u>.
   b <u>Quietly</u> the girl sat down.
5. a ask   b odd
6. Vicky got out her <u>book</u>.
7. a It's raining heavily. √
   b to accept punishment without complaint √
8. a clean   b dirty
9. a **be**friend b a**b**oard
10. <u>An owl</u> hunts at night .

Test 2 (pages 48 and 49)

1. a w**or**ld   b sw**ar**m
2. a Amy   b James
3. a accidenta**l** b rest**ful**
4. a "Where shall we go?" Charlotte asked.
   b Sarah replied, "Let's go shopping."
5. a swimming   b slipper
6. What is the capital of France?
7. a were   b was
8. a bus   b UK
9. a I stood at the front <u>so</u> I could see better.
   b I washed my hands <u>before</u> I ate my dinner.
10. a flint flour flush
    b broad brook brother

Test 3 (pages 50 and 51)

1. a match   b match
2. will skip   raked
3. a explo**sion**   b collec**tion**
4. a neatly   b enthusiastically
5. a short   b shout
6. a litter   b fleet
7. a to start afresh √
   b to be suspicious √
8.

root adjective	comparative form	superlative form
happy	happier	happiest
sad	sadder	saddest

9. a **for**give   b **ex**pand
10. a P   b S

Test 4 (pages 52 and 53)

1. a nothing   b front
2. a 2nd   b 3rd
3. a comfort   b child
4. a D   b R
5. a hoping   b manager
6. "Where's my towel, Amy?" Tom asked.
7. a I can't see any sweets.
   b I didn't hurt anyone.
8. a a kind of dance √
   b a musical instrument √
9. a Anna did not stop <u>although</u> she wanted to.
   b Anna rushed home <u>because</u> she was late.
10. a fleece   b gale